Come Sit with Me
Sermons for Children

Ron Miner

Illustrated by
Don-Paul Benjamin

The Pilgrim Press
Cleveland, Ohio

Acknowledgments

Without the assistance and inspiration of many people, this book would not have been possible. Special thanks and love to John Dennis, Deb DeMeester, Rob Elder, Bruce Gillette, Alice Godard, Fred Knickrehm, Barbara Moon, Jean Pokorny, and Barbara Price.

The Pilgrim Press, Cleveland, Ohio 44115

© 1981 by The Pilgrim Press

Biblical quotations, unless otherwise indicated, are from the Revised Standard Version of the Bible, © 1946, 1952, 1971, 1973 by the Division of Christian Education of the National Council of the Churches of Christ in the United States of America, and are used by permission. The biblical quotation marked JB is from The Jerusalem Bible, © 1966 by Darton, Longman and Todd, Ltd., and Doubleday and Company, Inc., and is used by permission of the publishers

Printed in the United States of America
The paper used in this publication is acid free and meets the minimum requirements of American National Standard for Information Sciences-Permanence of Paper for Printed Library Materials, ANSI Z39.48-1984

98 97 96 95 94 93   10 9 8 7 6 5 4 3

Library of Congress Cataloging-in-Publication Data

Miner, Ron, 1938-
        Come sit with me.
            1. Children's sermons. I. Title.
BV4315.M53   252'.53   81-10650
ISBN 0-8298-0469-2 (pbk.)   AACR2

Contents

Introduction

The future of the church we know and love lies in the younger generation, but all too often we fail to include the children at Sunday morning worship services. Children too need to hear—on their own level—the message of God's love for all people.

The sermons in this book are designed to appeal to children four to eight years old, but other children may participate. With appropriate modification, many of these sermons can be used for older youth. But everyone enters the sanctuary on Sunday morning as a child. If worship can involve the child in each of us, it is likely that the adult will be led to a personal relationship with God as well. One's age has nothing to do with ability to respond to the simple beauty of God's love. Were it otherwise, the parables of Jesus would never have survived.

Jesus called out to children that the disciples had sent away, and he declared: "Let the children come to me, and do not hinder them; for to such belongs the kingdom of God. Truly, I say to you, whoever does not receive the kingdom of God like a child shall not enter it [Luke 18:16-17]." The implications are twofold: (1) children do have a place in the Christian worship service and (2) a "sermon" or other presentation geared to children will remind everyone—adults included—of the beauty and simplicity of Christ's message.

Giving children's sermons can be a personal and intensely rewarding way to share the reality of Christian love. One can enjoy great freedom in presenting a brief experience to children. Having entered the sanctuary on stilts, skipped rope before the congregation, and blown soap bubbles in the house of God, I have experienced that freedom.

One hazard of putting these sermons in book form is that readers might think that these pages cover all the good ideas and that after the sermons are given another book is needed. But each person who fingers these pages has a background of his or her own unique holy experiences. Share those experiences in a way that is comfortable to you, and you will have enriched more than one life. Present them from the child in you to the "children" around you, and you will have given a children's sermon. Use the freedom you have to lead children of all ages to discover God's love in the world in which they live.

The children's sermons in this book were adapted from activities that took place on the chancel floor of the First Presbyterian Church in Corvallis, Oregon. The children are called forward about twenty minutes into the service. They sit on the floor with their backs to the congregation, and the leader sits on the floor with them. This establishes a sense of intimacy. A quality hand-held microphone is essential for the success of this system, because the rest of the congregation should be included. In a few weeks the children will be used to speaking into the microphone.

At the end of each sermon are noted "Materials" (prop/s needed) and "Scripture References" (thoughts for meditation) for use by the leader in preparing for the sermons.

The lesson plan for each sermon includes five basic steps:

1. *Motivation:* A presentation of materials, props, or concepts related to the sermon to set the stage and inspire interest.

2. *Activity:* A tangible experience in which the children can participate. The activity establishes a concrete basis for further discussion.

3. *Guided Discussion:* A period of discussion guided by the sermon leader. Includes key questions for the children to consider and anticipated responses.

4. *Leader Message:* A "script" for the leader with suggested statements. The message is designed to relate the children's experiences and discussion to Christian life.

5. *Closing Prayer:* A simple prayer that acknowledges the role of God in the topic of the session.

At the end of the sermon, the children may be dismissed to an alternate activity or to return to their families.

Who dares to write sermons for children? The child in me shares with the child in you, so that we both can celebrate our freedom. My freedom has come from the children who touch my life on a regular basis, the Kate, Sara, Fred, Betty, Warren, Rob, Kay, John, Fred, Don-Paul, and all other childlike souls that have shared with the child Ron.

Ron Miner

The Eye of the Beholder   God's Love

Motivation:	The leader places a large mirror on the floor and invites the children to sit around it.
Activity:	The leader invites the children to look in the mirror and asks them what they see. (Themselves.) The leader tells them to take a close look at themselves. How do they know who it is? How do they recognize themselves? (The children will probably point out obvious physical features like eye color, hair length/color, clothing they are wearing, etc.)

Guided
Discussion: The leader points out that these features are
                  certainly easy to see (recognize), but that
                  they don't really tell us much about the kind
                  of people we are: for example, they don't tell
                  us how nice we are or whether we love our
                  families.

Leader
Message: We can't really tell much about a person by
                  the way he or she looks. Each of us—each of
                  you—is special, not only because each of you
                  looks different, but also because of who you
                  are inside. God's love, the love inside of you,
                  is part of what makes each of you and each
                  person very special.
                      It takes more than just looking at the
                  outside to see the special effect God's love has
                  on you. Of course, we can't see inside one
                  another, but we can remember to do more
                  than just look at a person's outside. We can
                  take time to get to know people and to learn
                  about the love of God inside them and see
                  how beautiful they really are.

Closing
Prayer: Thank you, dear God, for having made each
                  of us different. Help us come to know the
                  beauty you have hidden inside us and inside
                  all your people. Amen.

Materials: Large wall mirror, framed or mounted on
                  wood for stability.

Scripture
References: 1 Corinthians 13:11-12
                  James 1:23-25

A Rose Is a Rose Is a Rose   God's Love

Motivation:

The leader gives each child a rose with a stem six to eight inches long.

Activity:

The children are invited to study their roses for a moment and be prepared to tell about them.

Guided
Discussion:

Tell me about your flower. (It's pretty. It's prickly. It has lots of leaves. It's colorful.) How does it smell? (It smells nice. It smells pretty.) We all seem to agree that the roses are beautiful and that we enjoy them. Did you notice that each rose has a stem? What happens if you squeeze the stem? (You get stuck with the thorns.) Isn't it interesting that as we talked about our roses no one complained about hurt hands. Maybe roses are so beautiful that we can overlook the thorns.

Leader
Message:

Roses aren't perfect. But they are so beautiful and so special that we tend to overlook their thorns. People are like that. We can love them even though they aren't perfect. We all have our thorns that make us hard to get along with and unpleasant at times. And yet those who care love us anyway. Think of how much God must love us—thorns and all. God loves each of us.

I want each of you to look around the church. Do you see someone who would enjoy receiving your rose as a token of God's love? I enjoyed giving each of you a rose. Now I want you to feel the joy of sharing your gift with someone else. Walk to that person now and give him or her your rose.

Closing Prayer:

We praise you, dear God, for the flowers of your creation. Help us to see the beauty that surrounds us, and help us to share that beauty. Thank you for loving us so much that our thorns don't overcome the beauty of your Spirit within us. Amen.

Materials: Long-stemmed roses in assorted colors.

Scripture References: Luke 13:6-9
Luke 15:1-7

No. 3

Measure for Measure   God's Love

Motivation: The leader displays two measuring utensils: a one-cup measure and a ¼ teaspoon measure.

Activity: The leader invites the children to think about how such items are used.

Guided Discussion: How are these things used? (To measure things. To cook.) Which one holds the most? (The cup.) Imagine all the delicious things this cup and spoon could hold. If someone were measuring out your favorite treat—chocolate or butterscotch or whipped cream—something you really wanted—would you want a spoonful or a cupful? (Cupful.)

Leader Message: God gives us something we want and need. God gives us love. God's love is poured all over us by the cupful, and here we are filled and overflowing with love.

How do we pass that love on to others? All too often, we pass on all that wonderful love using a very small spoon. Maybe we should be thankful that God gives us such a generous measure of love, and maybe we should be more generous when we pass that love on to others. Just think how empty we would feel if God used a spoon instead of a cup.

Closing Prayer: God, you love us far more than we can understand. Help us to accept the love you so freely give. Give us the courage to surprise others with our love. Amen.

Materials: One-cup measure; ¼ teaspoon measure.

Scripture Reference: 2 Corinthians 9:7

11

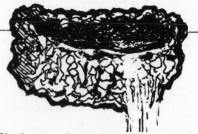

Getting in Shape
God's Love

Motivation: The leader displays a plastic basin, a pitcher of water, and a square of aluminum foil.

Activity: The leader says: "This morning I want you to recall a time when you were very thirsty. Think of how you longed for a drink of cool water. Will someone pour some water for me?" The leader holds the flat piece of foil in hand over the basin. The water poured from the pitcher runs off into the basin. The leader then shapes the foil into a cup. Now water poured collects in the foil cup. The leader drinks.

Guided Discussion: When the foil was flat what happened? (Water ran off.) When the foil was molded into the right shape what happened? (It held water. I was able to drink.)

Leader Message: We can think of the water as God's love. It is constantly poured out for us, but in order to receive it we need to prepare ourselves. We need to be in the right shape. One of the ways to get in shape is to come to church and worship God.

Closing Prayer: O God, shape our lives so we can accept your love, then help us to share that love with others. Amen.

Materials: Six-inch square of aluminum foil; pitcher of water; plastic basin.

Scripture Reference: Colossians 2:6

No. 5

Among the Living   God's Love

Motivation: The leader displays three tree twigs: one from which all the leaves have fallen, one with only dry, autumn-colored leaves, and one with fresh green leaves.

Activity: The twigs are passed around for each child's inspection. The leader asks which of the twigs came from a living tree. (The green one. The one with all the good leaves.)

Guided
Discussion: We all seem to think the twig with the green leaves comes from a living tree, but what about the others? In fact, each of these twigs came from a living tree. When we look closely at the twigs without green leaves, we can see small signs of life. What are these called? (Buds. Flowers. Blossoms.)

Leader
Message: These twigs all came from living trees. They each represent a different time or season in the tree's life, but they are all part of that life.

In autumn the trees shed their leaves to prepare for winter. The buds remain as promises of life. The green leaves come forth in the spring and summer.

There are times in our lives when the usual signs of joy—the green leaves—are hard to find. We feel unhappy and empty. At such times we must trust in God, remembering that as a tree has its seasons, so our lives are full of ups and downs. But God's promise of life is with us all the time, and we can see it if we look carefully.

Closing Prayer: O God, your power and love are seen in all creation. Help us to see and feel your love and your promise of life. Amen.

Materials: Three twigs, one with green leaves, one with autumn leaves, one from which all the leaves have fallen.

Scripture Reference: Mark 4:26-28

Something to Share God's Love

Motivation: The leader says "Imagine this morning that you are crossing a hot desert. All you can think of is how much you want a drink of water. Just in case we find some, each of you will need a paper cup." Each child receives a small paper cup.

Activity: The children are led a short distance to where three thermoses have been placed: two empty and one filled with water. "Ah, we seem to have found what we need!" The first two thermoses prove a disappointment. The third has water, and all the cups are filled. "Let's drink the water." The group returns to the discussion area, where the cups are disposed of.

Guided Discussion: How did you feel when you didn't get any water? (Cheated. Disappointed. You fooled us.)

Leader Message: This was not just an exercise in looking for water. People are always looking for something more precious than water. They are looking for love.

When they look for love, they turn to other people. Sometimes they find that other people have nothing to share, like the first two thermoses. At other times, they meet people who have God's love in them. This is love everyone can share.

It is important that we fill ourselves with God's love so we have something to share with others.

Closing Prayer: God, it is good to have a love that we can share with others. Fill us with your love, so that all who seek love and caring can find refreshment in us. Amen.

Materials: Three thermoses; paper cups; wastebasket.

Scripture Reference: 1 John 4:16b, 19

No. 7

Keep Swinging   Forgiveness

Motivation: The leader produces a baseball glove and bat.

Activity: The children are invited to take up certain baseball positions: catcher, batter, etc. The leader is the pitcher. Once everyone is in position, the leader pretends to pitch an imaginary ball. The batter is allowed three swings, each called a strike, and is called out. The materials are then collected and the children assemble for discussion.

Guided Discussion: When I said "You're out!" what did that mean? (Your turn has ended. You must sit down.) That's bad news, isn't it? When we strike out, we can't play anymore—we lose our turn.

Leader Message: Each time we swing at the ball, we do our best. We try to hit it, but sometimes we fail. That sort of thing happens in real life too. No matter how hard we may try to do something right, we miss.

In baseball we get three strikes. How many strikes do we get in life? (Various ideas.) Well, I'm happy to report that God tells us to keep swinging. God forgives us if we make strikes. That's part of the good news of God's love: We can keep striking without being called out.

Closing Prayer: Dear God, we thank you for loving us even when we don't do what you want. Help us to love others at all times, even when they do things we don't like. Amen.

Materials: Baseball glove and bat.

Scripture Reference: Matthew 18:21, 22

17

A Missing Treasure   Forgiveness

Motivation: The leader produces the classified-ad section of a newspaper.

Activity: The children listen as the leader reads two or three lost pet ads.

Guided Discussion: Why do you suppose the people who own these pets went to all the trouble of looking for them? (Love them. Miss them.) Let's suppose you had two dogs and you loved them both. If one got lost would you say, "Well, that's too bad, but I still have one dog left," or would you try to find the lost pet? (Look for it.)

Leader
Message: Jesus tells a story about a shepherd who went
                in search of a lost sheep. Even though this
                shepherd had many other sheep, he left them
                all to look for the one that had strayed away.
                The lost sheep was probably not an especially
                beautiful sheep, but the shepherd loved it.
                     God's love and God's forgiveness are like
                that. We are all special to God, and if even
                one of us strays, God reaches out to find us.

Closing
Prayer: Dear God, because we know you love us, we
                feel safe and secure. Help us to stay close to
                you, so we can feel the warmth of your caring.
                Amen.

Materials: Newspaper classified-ad section containing
                lost pet announcements.

Scripture
Reference: Matthew 18:12-14

Pen or Pencil?   Forgiveness

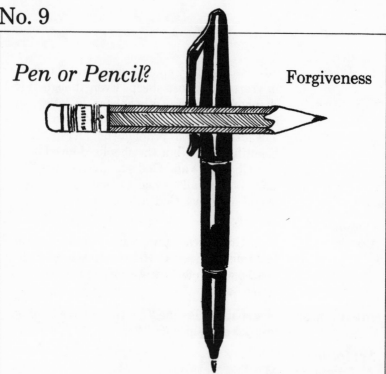

Motivation:	The leader displays a large blank piece of paper on an easel.
Activity:	Two or three children are invited to come forward and make a large "X" on the paper. Some children are given pencils. Others are given pens.
Guided Discussion:	Which of these marks can be easily erased? (The pencil marks.) Which will be left when I erase? (The pen marks. The ink.)
Leader Message:	As we pass through life, each of us leaves marks, signs that we have been here. We leave footprints in the snow and sand. We write things in school. We send letters to

friends. Those things which we hope will last, we usually write in ink. Those things which we want to be able to change, or which are not too important, we usually write in pencil.

Each day offers us many choices. Sometimes we choose to act in ways that we know are pleasing to God, sometimes we don't. I like to think that our good actions are written in ink and those things which we might have done better are written in pencil. When we accept Jesus, we allow him to cleanse our lives by erasing our mistakes and by making our successes even more special.

Closing
Prayer: Dear God, we thank you for Jesus who takes away our sins. Help us to leave, in ink, a permanent record of a life devoted to you. Amen.

Materials: Large sheet of paper mounted on an easel; pencils and pens.

Scripture
Reference: Colossians 3:12-13

Cycle, Cycle, Recycle   Forgiveness

Motivation: The leader displays a bushel basket containing aluminum soft-drink cans, a newspaper, and a brown-glass syrup jar.

Activity: The children are invited to examine the items in the basket and to decide if they can be used again or must be thrown away.

Guided Discussion: Should we throw these things away? (No.) Why? (They can be reused/recycled. They are still good.) All these things can be recycled. They can be used again and again. Who do you think first had the idea of recycling things? (Various guesses.)

Leader Message: I believe *God* first had the idea of recycling. God recognized that people, the earth's greatest resource, were not living good lives. God sent Jesus, God's son, to teach us and to

give his life so that we could be recycled into a better life.

This is the good news that Jesus represents. We are not doomed to be thrown away. We can be recycled into fuller and richer lives by accepting Jesus as our Savior.

Closing
Prayer:

Jesus, thank you for helping to redirect our lives. Because of you, all people, our most important resources, are recycled and saved. May we be worthy of your love. Amen.

Materials:

Bushel basket; aluminum soft-drink cans; a newspaper; brown-glass syrup jar.

Scripture
Reference:

Matthew 6:12

Along Came a Spider   Forgiveness

Motivation: The leader produces a large jar or dry aquarium that is laced with spider webs.

Activity: The children are invited to examine the display and to think about how the webs look.

Guided Discussion: Is a web like a window? In what way? (We can see through it.) Is a web like a net? In what way? (It is hooked together.) What is the purpose of a web? (To catch insects for a spider to eat.)

Leader Message:	A web is really a combination of a window and a net. It is nearly transparent—which means we have to look closely to see it. It is almost invisible. If we look closely, though, we find that the web is hooked together by tiny threads. In this way it is like a net. The spider uses the web as a net to catch insects for food.
	Sin is something like a spider's web. This is not to say that spiders are sinful or that webs are evil. But the web does give us a way of looking at sin and a way of thinking about it. Although sin is usually very easy to see, it is sometimes pretty sneaky. It is a trap, a net waiting to catch those who are lost.
	But Jesus reminds us that if we follow him and believe in him we will not be lost and our sins will be forgiven. Jesus helps us escape the web of sin.
Closing Prayer:	God, help us to be strong, to resist the temptations of this world. Help us to do your will always. Amen.
Materials:	Large jar or dry aquarium that is laced with spider webs. It is best to leave the spider out of the jar or aquarium.
Scripture *Reference:*	Psalm 31:4

Best Vessels

Communion

Motivation: The leader displays cups made from a variety of materials—paper, Styrofoam, china.

Activity: The children are invited to inspect the cups and to think about why each is made of a different material, then the cups are collected.

Guided Discussion: Which of these cups would be best for hot liquids? (The Styrofoam cup or the china cup.) Which is used mostly for cold drinks? (The paper cup.) Which is most likely to break when dropped? (The china cup.)

Leader Message: Although each of these cups serves the same purpose—to hold liquids we drink—each is best to use for a certain type of liquid. The Bible talks about *people* as being cups or containers too. People who are prepared to hear God's word are like a cup that has been made to hold the right kind of liquid. God's message is for those who are ready to hear it and to hold it (here the leader might cup his or her hands to illustrate) just as a cup holds water or coffee.

We make ourselves ready to receive God's wonderful message by coming to church, by studying the Bible, and—as we are doing today—receiving communion. As we take communion, we think of it as a special way of preparing to hear and hold God's message.

Closing
Prayer: Thank you, God, for the gift of communion. Help us to be ready to receive the power and joy of your word. May we each be cups suitable to receive the loving flow of your message. Amen.

Materials: Cups made of paper, Styrofoam, and china.

Scripture
Reference: Matthew 26:26-28

More Bounce per Ounce Christian Spirit

Motivation: The leader displays a severely underinflated basketball which is held carefully so that its condition is not apparent. "What will happen if I drop this ball?" (It will bounce.)

Activity: The leader drops the ball and it lands with a dull thud. The leader then produces a tire pump, inflates the ball, bounces it to produce the desired result, and then places the ball and pump to one side.

Guided Discussion: Why didn't the ball bounce the first time? (No air. It was flat.) What did I do? (Pumped it up. Added air.) Why is it important for a ball to bounce? (So it will be useful. So you can play with it.)

Leader Message: The ball was not useful or much fun when it was flat. It lacked bounce. Sometimes people, groups of people—even churches—become like our ball. In order to put the bounce back into our ball, we needed something inside: air.

When people lose their bounce—when they lose their excitement for life—they need something inside too. For people, that something is love; for the church it is the spirit of God's love. People and churches need this inner spirit in order to be alive and caring and giving.

Closing
Prayer:

O God, inflate us with your love. We, like balls, can become flat, but with your love, we can recover fullness of life. Amen.

Materials:

Ball (a small playground ball may be preferable to a basketball since it will take less time to pump up); a tire pump.

Scripture
Reference:

2 Timothy 1:7

Thinking Positive   Christian Spirit

Motivation: The leader displays two or three sheets of white cardboard on each of which have been mounted a photograph of the leader and its negative.

Activity: The sheets are passed around for the children to inspect. They are asked to think about which of the two images on each sheet looks most like the leader.

Guided Discussion: (Displaying one of the sheets.) Which of these two images looks most like me? (The black-and-white one. The shiny one. The larger one [see materials note below]). What is this other thing called? (A negative.)

Leader Message: We seem to agree that the black-and-white photograph looks more like me than the negative. The photograph is sometimes called a *positive*. In school, at home, and in church we hear a lot of talk about positive attitudes. When we have a positive attitude we are happy. We think things will work out well.

We share our happiness. When our attitude is negative, we are sad, even angry. We make others feel sad and angry too. We always think the worst will happen when our attitude is negative.

Every once in a while, it's a good idea to remind ourselves about positive and negative attitudes. As Christians—filled with the spirit of Jesus—we try to have positive attitudes. This is as it should be, because we are more like ourselves when we are positive than when we are negative.

Closing
Prayer:

Dear God, fill us with the spirit and joy of Jesus, that we may be positive people and may add to the greatness of your kingdom. Amen.

Materials: Two or three white cardboard sheets on each of which have been mounted a photograph of the leader and its corresponding negative. To assist the children in identifying the image that looks most like the leader, it will be best if the positive is somewhat larger than the negative.

Scripture
References: Galatians 5:22-23a, 25
Philippians 4:8

Out of Sight   Faith

Motivation: The leader produces a cardboard box that has been securely taped shut. The leader announces that an object has been placed inside.

Activity: As the leader tips the box back and forth, the children are invited to listen closely and see

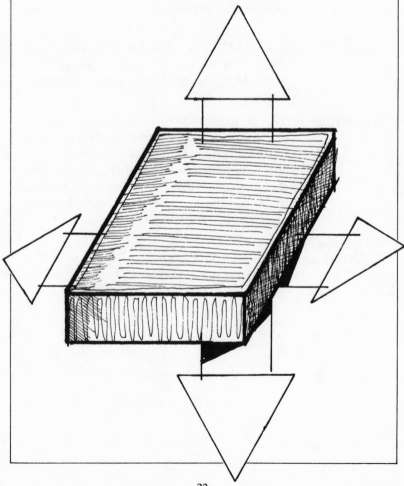

	if they can guess what the object is by the sound it makes.
Guided Discussion:	What do you think is inside? (Various guesses.) How can we find out for certain? (Open the box. Look inside.) You have all made good guesses and you are probably very curious about what really is inside. But I am purposely not going to open this box. (The box is put away.)
Leader Message:	We hear a lot about faith in church. Do we really know what it means? Suppose someone whom you trusted told you what was inside that box. If you really trusted that person and believed in what he or she said, you wouldn't have to look in the box. You would know the person spoke the truth and your curiosity would be satisfied.
	Keeping our faith is difficult. Keeping our faith means trusting and believing in the answers which God gives us. (As an example of this message, the leader should now tell the children what is in the box, but not open the box.)
Closing Prayer:	Dear God, give us the faith to believe in what we cannot see. Amen.
Materials:	Cardboard box similar in size and shape to a donut or pastry box; any object that would make a distinctive sound when put in the closed box and moved around.
Scripture Reference:	Hebrews 11:1, 3

33

No. 16

That Special Glow
Faith

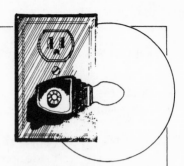

Motivation: The leader displays a night-light.

Activity: The children are invited to think about why the night-light is so special.

Guided
Discussion: Why is this light special? (Helps you see in the dark. Helps little kids sleep better. Nice to wake up and see it. Makes the dark nicer.)

Leader
Message: A night-light is special. It can be a reminder that everything is OK. We wake up from a dream and see it shining and go peacefully back to sleep. It makes the night seem a lot more friendly.

As Christians, we depend on another special glow too. This glow, which is inside us, is called *faith*. Our faith in God and in Jesus makes us feel warm inside and helps us face the difficult things that are part of life.

Let's all sit quietly for a moment with our eyes closed and imagine that warm Christian glow deep inside us—that special night-light—that comes from faith. Feel it glowing? Isn't that a nice feeling?

Closing
Prayer: Thank you, God, for the warm glow of faith. Strengthen our faith and guide us to do your will. Amen.

Materials: Child's night-light.
Scripture
Reference: John 8:12

Piecework   Faith

Motivation:	The leader displays a small puzzle that appears to have been assembled upside down. Two or three pieces are not yet in place.
Activity:	Two or three children are invited to come forward and put in the remaining pieces.
Guided Discussion:	What is different about this puzzle? (It's upside down. You've got the wrong side up.) Why is it harder to put a puzzle together when it's upside down? (Can't see the picture. Nothing to look at. Can't see the colors. Can't see how it goes together.)
Leader Message:	Much of what happens in our lives is very puzzling. People we care about get hurt. We ourselves get sick. Sometimes we're very happy, at other times we can't keep from crying. We hurt people's feelings when we don't mean to, and they yell at us even though we know they don't mean it. It's all hard to understand.
	Unless we have *faith* that God has a plan for us, and unless we live the way God wants us to, things seem to be very confusing. Here's how faith works: *We* put the pieces of our lives together working on the back side. From God's point of view the picture looks fine, but from our side it's just a puzzle. Still, if we do God's will, things seem to fit. Even

when we're finished, it may not look quite right, but our faith tells us that if we live our lives as God wants us to, we'll make a beautiful life.

Faith is like working on the dull downside of the puzzle (the leader places a flat cardboard on top of the upside-down puzzle), but knowing all along that on the other side (the leader flips the puzzle over and displays an attractive landscape to the children) is a beautiful picture.

Closing
Prayer:

We have faith, God, that your plan for our lives is the best plan. Help us to bear the uncertainties and to deal with the confusion, that we may live our lives in a way which reflects your will. Amen.

Materials:

Small puzzle of an attractive landscape; two pieces of stiff cardboard slightly larger than the assembled puzzle. In preparing for the sermon, the puzzle is first assembled faceup on one piece of stiff cardboard. It is important that the puzzle and cardboards be no larger than a foot square for ease in handling. To flip the puzzle over, place the second cardboard on top of the puzzle. This will form a sandwich that keeps the assembled puzzle together. Holding one hand under the bottom cardboard and the other on top of the upper cardboard, the puzzle can be flipped either way without disturbing the pieces. The biggest challenge will be displaying the puzzle to the children, since it must be kept in a horizontal position lest the pieces slide off the board.

Scripture
Reference: Jeremiah 29:11

Plain Brown Wrapper
Christian Potential

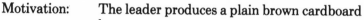

Motivation:	The leader produces a plain brown cardboard box.
Activity:	The children are invited to think of ways they could use the box, either as a toy or for practical purposes.
Guided Discussion:	How might you use this box? (Make a house. Carry things. Make a rocketship. Store things.) Cardboard is a fascinating thing. It is very ordinary, but we can think of a number of ways to use it. We all have plans to make it into something useful and something special.
Leader Message:	God has special plans for each of us. Just as we were able to think of many special uses for this box, each of us is capable of doing very special things. God knows how special we are and how each of us can be useful and helpful. Through God's love we experience all that we can be.
Closing Prayer:	O God, what magnificent plans do you have for us? Open us up to new possibilities, so that we may serve you in new and exciting ways. Amen.
Materials:	Medium-sized cardboard box without lettering. If a more dramatic effect is desired a larger, refrigerator-sized box might be used.
Scripture Reference:	Philippians 2:13

The Good Earth   Christian Potential

Motivation:	The leader displays a shallow pan in which soil has been packed. Half the soil is damp and rich-looking, the other half is dry and brittle.
Activity:	Two or three children are chosen to come forward, take some seeds from a bag, and place them in the soil where they will have the best chance of growing.
Guided Discussion:	Which soil is the best place for seeds to grow? (The dark dirt. The wet side.) Why? (The seeds need good dirt. Need water.) What is wrong with this other dirt? (It's too dry. It's not good. Not wet.)
Leader Message:	Jesus told a story in the Bible. He compared the word of God to a seed. He said that if a seed is planted in good soil it will grow. The people who heard this story were confused. When they asked Jesus to explain it, he said that people who hear the word of God and take it in are like the good soil. The

seed of God's word will grow in those who hear and believe.

Wouldn't it be wonderful if the word of God could take root in everyone? Think of what a beautiful garden we'd make!

Closing
Prayer:

Dear God, thank you for your wonderful word. Help us to be good soil, ready for planting and firm in our Christian growth. Amen.

Materials:

Cake pan or other shallow pan; rich, damp soil and poor, dry soil; seeds.

Scripture
Reference:

Matthew 13:23

The Church That Works Together   The Christian Church

Motivation:	The leader spreads a canvas on the floor and dumps a pile of dry soil in the middle. The leader produces a whisk broom and plucks a single straw for each child.
Activity:	The leader holds a dustpan and asks the children to sweep the dirt into it. As they work at this task they may complain. (It won't work. We can't do it. These are too small. Too weak.) After a few moments, the leader produces the whisk broom and quickly sweeps the dirt into the dustpan.
Guided Discussion:	Ask the children to discuss their problem. (We didn't have enough straws. Our straws were too small.) How was the problem solved? (The leader used the whole broom.) By themselves, the straws from the whisk broom couldn't clean up the dirt. No matter how hard we tried, we couldn't move things. The whisk broom—which is a lot of straws working together—was able to do the job.

Leader	
Message:	This adventure with the whisk broom and the straws tells us something about our church and its members. When we work together, the members of the church can do things as a group which they cannot do separately, as individuals. By being together and working together we can do things that are impossible for us when we try alone.
	In the case of the whisk broom, many straws are held together by strings and glue. In the case of our church, many people—the members of our church—are held together by God's love. God's love binds us together and helps us work together to do good things.
Closing	
Prayer:	O God, strengthen our efforts with your love. We feel weak and alone when separated from your presence. Bind us together, that we might better serve you. Amen.
Materials:	Whisk broom; dry earth (potting soil is best); canvas cloth or drop cloth.
Scripture	
References:	1 Corinthians 3:12-15
	Romans 12:4-5

The Tie That Binds The Christian Church

Motivation: The leader produces a rope and asks each child to take a position along its length. (The rope should be of sufficient length so that all children can find a place.)

Activity: Each child grasps the rope and follows as the leader takes the children for a short walk around a section of the sanctuary. When the group returns to the starting point, the children sit in a circle with the rope encircled on the floor in front of them.

Guided
Discussion: Ask the children to discuss their walk. Did anyone get lost on our walk? (No.) Did anyone fall down? (No.) What was special about our walk? (We were together. We walked together.) The rope kept us from getting lost or separated from the group. If anyone had stumbled, the rest of us could have helped that person. When we walk together, we depend on one another. We are joined together.

Leader Message:	Try to imagine a rope long enough for everyone in our church to hold. Everyone in our town. How about a very long rope, a rope long enough so that everybody in the world could walk together as we have walked today?
	Jesus' love is like that—a rope, a tie that binds all people together. Jesus' love helps people everywhere to walk together without getting lost, without stumbling. Just as our small group is joined together by this rope, so all Christians are joined together. We are all part of the one Christ, Jesus, and we are all tied together by Jesus' love.
Closing Prayer:	Dear God, we thank you for the love that binds us to one another, keeps us from falling, and reminds us that we do not walk alone. Help us to cling to your love and make it part of our lives. Amen.
Materials:	Length of rope. A cord such as that used in swimming pools or as a divider in theater lobbies might be best. A regular rope has burrs that may injure small hands.
Scripture References:	John 15:1-5
	Romans 8:38-39

Standing Together The Christian Church

Motivation: The leader gives each child a three-inch length of rope.

Activity: The children are directed to stand their piece of rope on end. The leader attempts this and invites the children to try. After a few moments, the leader collects the lengths and binds them together with two or three rubber bands. Bound together, the ropes can easily be stood on end.

Guided Discussion: What happened when we tried to stand each rope up by itself? (Each fell over.) Why? (Too weak. Couldn't balance. Too flimsy.) Did you notice how, when bound together with rubber bands, the ropes stood nicely?

Leader Message: Although the rubber bands did not hold the ropes up, they did bind the ropes together in such a way that they supported one another. Bound together, the ropes could do something they couldn't do alone.

We can think of each piece of rope as a person. When many people are bound together, they can accomplish things as a group they could never do alone. We are bound together in a church. We are bound together by the love of God. God's love makes us solid and helps us support one another.

Closing Prayer: O God, your love binds us together so that we cannot fall. Help us to support and care for one another as you support and care for us. Amen.

Materials: Ten or more three-inch lengths of rope; two or three thick rubber bands.

Scripture Reference: Matthew 18:20

Coming Attractions The Christian Church

Motivation:	The leader displays a large horseshoe magnet and a flat cardboard covered with thick but transparent acetate. The acetate-covered cardboard has some iron filings inside. The cardboard is mounted on an easel so that it is visible to the congregation.
Activity:	The leader invites two or three children forward to manipulate the magnet so that the iron filings are drawn to it as it is passed over the face of the acetate.
Guided Discussion:	What sorts of things does this magnet pull to it? (Paper clips. Nails. Other metal objects.) Does it attract cloth? (No—demonstrate if appropriate.) Does it attract paper? (No.)

Leader Message:	This magnet attracts metal. The magnet is metal itself, but it is energized with a special force called magnetism. Some people are like that—energized. You like them instantly. They are pleasant to be around. They are fun and exciting. They have the ability to attract other people. This ability is also called magnetism. What is this magic energy that attracts people? Often, it is the fact that they are Christians. As Christians, we have a special spirit, a special glow, a special energy which comes from knowing that Jesus is our Savior and that God loves us. Let's all try to be magnets and draw others into the love of Jesus.
Closing Prayer:	We pray, dear God, that we may draw others closer to Jesus through our example. Amen.
Materials:	Large horseshoe magnet and an acetate-covered piece of cardboard. Iron filings and an easel. Be certain to test the magnet before using and to follow proper care in storing prior to use so that its magnetism is not weakened.
Scripture *Reference:*	1 John 4:7

Full House — The Christian Church

Motivation: The leader displays a large movie poster.

Activity: The poster is put to one side and the children are invited to think about what they do when they go to the movies.

Guided
Discussion: What happens before you can get into the movie? What do you need? (Must buy a ticket.) What do you do when you first get

inside? (Get some popcorn/soda. Give your tickets to the ticket-taker. Go to the bathroom.) When it is time to pick a seat, how do you decide where to sit? (Sit in the middle. Need enough seats for everyone. Don't sit behind tall people. Sit near the front.)

Leader
Message:

Have you ever noticed that there are sometimes empty seats in church? Most of us would probably prefer that every seat be filled. I've given a lot of thought to these empty seats, and I'm not convinced that every seat should be taken.

In some Christian groups the people join hands when they pray, but when they join hands they always leave a space for someone who should be there but isn't. I like to think of an empty seat in church as a reminder of those people we wish were here to worship with us. Maybe we should each invite someone to visit our church and to join us in our celebration of God.

Closing
Prayer:

God, help us to think of you every day, not just on Sundays. Remind us at work or at school that there are others who would like to know you better. Guide us to invite others to join us as we worship you. Amen.

Materials:

Movie poster that would appeal to children, perhaps a Walt Disney or science fiction feature. It will be a challenge to keep the children from telling the plot of the movie, so be certain to put this prop out of view after it has served as motivation.

*Scripture
Reference:*

2 Corinthians 5:20a

A Well-built Quilt   The Christian Church

Motivation: The leader displays a patchwork quilt.

Activity: The children are invited to examine the quilt and to think about how it was made.

Guided
Discussion: How was this quilt made? (Many small patches were sewn together. People sewed it.) Why are there so many different designs? (Not enough of one fabric to make a whole blanket. To make it more interesting/ prettier.)

Leader
Message: This quilt is a collection of many different patterns and designs. Together these small

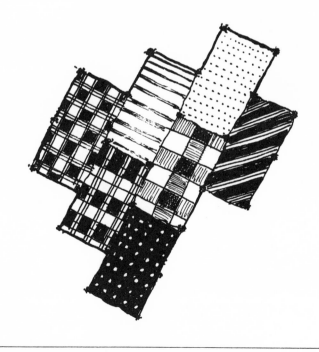

bits of cloth make a beautiful and useful blanket. This is like what happens when the people of a church join together in fellowship. Women, men, and children all gather together to share God's love. When they do this an exciting thing happens. Turn around for a moment and look at our congregation. See how they resemble a beautiful quilt—different faces, different colors, individual people, but all united in their love for God and for one another.

Closing Prayer:

God, we thank you for inviting us to join together in fellowship. It is you who have designed and fashioned this beautiful patchwork of people we call our congregation. Grant that we may love and cherish one another as you love each of us. Amen.

Materials: Patchwork quilt.

Scripture Reference: Romans 12:4-5

Growing Wings   The Christian Journey

Motivation:	The leader unveils an aquarium from which the water has been emptied. Inside are two or three chrysalises of the monarch butterfly.
Activity:	Each child is invited to describe what he or she sees. (Bugs. Cocoons.)
Guided Discussion:	These motionless mysteries are called chrysalises or, as some of you called them, cocoons. What's inside? (A bug. Worm. Caterpillar. Butterfly.) This creature began as an egg, then it became a larva or caterpillar, now it is a chrysalis. What comes next? (Becomes a butterfly. Becomes a flying insect.)
Leader Message:	At each stage in its life the butterfly looks different and lives in a different way. People go through stages and changes too. We start out as babies, we spend a few wonderful years

as children, then we become teenagers, and finally we become grown-ups. Many of us who are older would like a chance to do it all over again. At each stage in our life, we look different and we act differently.

The Bible tells us that God expects different things from us as we grow. One reason we come to church is to learn how God wants us to live. The more we learn, the closer we come to growing our own wings.

Closing
Prayer:

God, as we grow, the promise of your love throughout our lives gives us the hope of even more wonderful days to come. Give us a glimpse of the beauty that is possible in life with you. Amen.

Materials: Aquarium with two or three chrysalises of the monarch butterfly, a cloth cover.

Scripture
Reference: Ephesians 4:15-16

Part One: Great Expectations

The Christian Journey

Motivation:
The leader displays a goldfish bowl. The children are told that the leader is going to plant a winter garden.

Activity:
As the children watch, the leader places a few solid objects in the bowl and pours a solution over the objects so that each is wet (see materials listed below). The objects are then coated with salt, and a few drops of red and yellow food coloring are splashed at various points on the pile.

Guided
Discussion:
(None today.)

Leader
Message:
As I have been working here in silence, you have—by your attention—preached a powerful sermon. By the way you watched, I can tell that each of you is expecting something to happen.

When we come to church, we should come expecting things to happen. We should expect to see and talk with people who care about us. We should expect to hear things that help us grow in our love and understanding of God. And we should expect to learn from our worship. We should also expect to change, not only while we are in church, but during the time from one worship service to the next.

Next time we meet, we'll take another look at our winter garden. It has already begun to change, but the changes are so tiny that you can't see them. Next week you'll see some very exciting changes. In the meantime, think about this experience, and about the other things that happened in church today. Carry them with you as you grow during the coming week.

Closing Prayer: Dear God, help us to expect great things of our church. Instill in us a sense of wonder and excitement as we worship in your name. Amen.

Materials: Medium-size goldfish bowl. A few solid objects such as lumps of charcoal, a piece of sponge, stones, short sticks, or tree bark. Salt and red and yellow food coloring. A solution of 3 tablespoons salt, 3 tablespoons household ammonia, 3 tablespoons household bluing, and 6 tablespoons water. Utensils to dispense the ingredients, including an eyedropper for the food coloring, will be helpful. The solution will cause crystals to form. (Experiment ahead of time to achieve best results.)

Scripture Reference: 2 Corinthians 5:17

Part Two: How Does Your Garden Grow?

The Christian Journey

Motivation:	The leader displays the developed winter garden.
Activity:	The children are invited to inspect the garden.
Guided Discussion:	How did our garden look last week? (It was plain. Not pretty. Just a pile of wet stuff.) How does it look now? (Pretty. Nice. Like flowers. Like a garden.)

Leader Message:

During the week, there have been many changes in our winter garden. It changed from an unattractive collection of wet things into a colorful bowl of crystals.

It took time for this to happen. We have all changed since last week. We've grown a little older, of course, but we've grown inside too. That's what happens when God touches our lives. In addition to growing on the outside like everyone else, we—as Christians—change in other ways. Inside of us, love and trust and faith grow stronger. These beautiful parts of our lives begin with our love and trust and faith in God, then—just as with our winter garden—such things grow more and more beautiful with each passing day.

Closing Prayer:

Dear God, thank you for love and trust and faith. Make us a fertile garden where such things can grow and prosper. Amen.

Materials: Winter garden "planted" last session.

Scripture Reference: 2 Corinthians 9:8

Something in the Air   The Holy Spirit

Motivation: The leader produces a bubble wand and blows a few bubbles.

Activity: Two or three of the children are invited to blow a few bubbles. As the last child's bubbles float away, the materials are put aside.

Guided
Discussion: What did you do to make the bubbles? (We blew them. Air.) What would happen if I held this bubble-maker up in the wind outside? Would it make more bubbles? (Yes.)

Leader
Message: The movement of air—the blowing of air—is called wind. Wind makes the trees sway. It

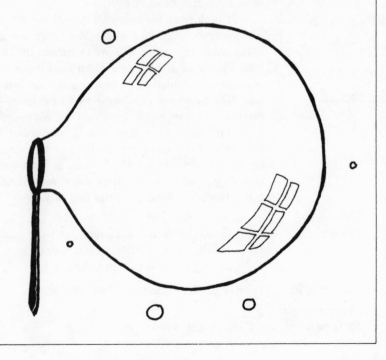

makes sailboats move. It makes waves on a lake. The wind is there, that's for certain. We can't actually see the wind, but we can see what it does and we can feel it moving around us.

The Bible mentions a different kind of wind. As a matter of fact, the Bible was first written in another language, and in that language the word for wind is the same as the word for spirit. So wind and the idea of spirit are much alike.

In church, we talk about a special kind of wind that touches us; we call it the Holy Spirit. The touch of the Holy Spirit is difficult to explain, just as it is difficult to explain the wind. Once a person feels the wind of the Holy Spirit, that person can never be the same. This is one of the great mysteries and great truths of our religion.

Closing
Prayer: Dear God, thank you for the truth of the Holy Spirit. We pray that we may grow in understanding of this and all your wonderful mysteries. Amen.

Materials: Bubble wand (preferable to a bubble pipe, since children don't have to place the wand in their mouth to blow bubbles); bubble solution.

Scripture
Reference: Acts 2:1-4

And Now a Word from . . . Christian Witness

Motivation:	The leader displays a can of dog food.
Activity:	The children are invited to pretend that they are television announcers. Their job is to say a few words about this wonderful dog food so that people watching television will want to buy it. Two children (volunteers) are asked to deliver brief commercials. If no one volunteers, the leader should be prepared to make a testimonial. The materials are then put aside.
Guided Discussion:	Why do we have commercials on television? (To pay for the shows.)

Leader Message:

Television commercials are often a nuisance, but they do help pay for the programs we enjoy. Television isn't the only place we see commercials. Every day we meet new people. Every person we meet is a walking commercial for something. Some tell us, "I'm lost. Come with me and be lost too." Others say, "I'm sad," or "I'm angry. You should feel that way too." Some say, "I'm a Christian. Try it, you'll like it."

I wonder what sort of advertisements or commercials we are for Christ. Do people know just by meeting us that we represent the most wonderful sponsor in the universe?

Closing Prayer:

Thank you, dear God, for sponsoring us, for believing in us, and for loving us. We pray that we may be worthy of your love. Amen.

Materials: Can of dog food.

Scripture Reference: Colossians 3:16-17

Brushing Up   Prayer

Motivation: The leader displays a large toothbrush and a
                set of teeth.

Activity: The children are invited to come forward and
                demonstrate proper brushing technique.
                After one or two have done so, the materials
                are put aside.

Guided
Discussion: How often should you brush? (At least once
                each day. Preferably after every meal.) Why
                do we brush our teeth? (To keep them
                healthy. Prevent cavities. Remove food.)
                What would happen if we didn't brush?
                (Would get cavities. Teeth would decay, rot,
                fall out.)

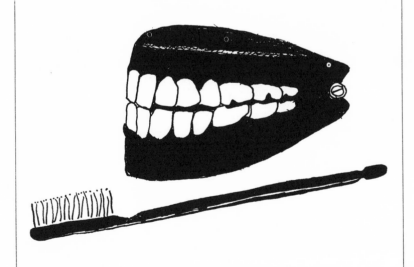

Leader Message:	Brushing your teeth regularly is like praying. We pray for much the same reason we brush our teeth: to keep our Christian spirit healthy and to prevent cavities from forming in our soul. If we don't pray, our souls tend to suffer. Let's all try to remember to brush, and pray, regularly.
Closing Prayer:	Dear God, help us to remember that prayer is important. Lead us to pray more often and to turn to you in times of sadness and in times of joy. In Jesus' name we pray. Amen.
Materials:	A large toothbrush and a set of teeth. These might be borrowed from a local children's dentist, from a public health center, or from a school.
Scripture Reference:	John 15:4-5

A Joyful Noise

Prayer

Motivation:	The leader displays a tape recorder. A tape featuring a series of noises is in place in the machine.
Activity:	The children listen to the tape and try to remember as many sounds as they can.
Guided Discussion:	What sounds did you hear? (Various answers.) Which sound was the loudest? (Various answers.)
Leader Message:	I want you to help me make the loudest, most powerful sound I know. I want you and the rest of the congregation to join me in a moment of silent prayer. Let us pray. (Leader, children, and the rest of the congregation pray silently for a few moments.) Amen.

There are many sounds in this world: horns honk, cars roar, dogs bark, thunder booms, and teakettles whistle. Sometimes all this noise causes us to pay too much attention to what's going on in the world. When that happens, we may forget about God and about the powerful voice of prayer. The next

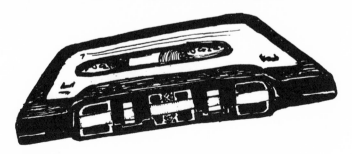

time you pray, remember that—of all the sounds—prayer is the most pleasing to God.

Closing Prayer:
We thank you, dear God, for the gift of prayer. Help us to keep our attention focused on the importance of rising above the noise of the world. Let our prayers be a joyful noise, praising you. Amen.

Materials:
Tape recorder; tape of familiar sounds: car starting, animal sounds, siren, thunder, and so on. A local radio station might be contacted to obtain a sound effects record for recording purposes.

Scripture Reference:
Matthew 6:6

A Book for All Ages The Bible

Motivation: The leader produces a cloth bag or a box. One by one various books are shown to the children: a thick and forbidding hardbound novel, a child's picture book, a school reader, and a Bible.

Activity: As the children examine each book, the leader invites them to think about the type of person who might be able to read it.

Guided
Discussion: Who might read this large book? (A smart person. An older person. A grown-up.) How about this school book? (Second-grader. It's like my books.) Who would enjoy this picture book? (My little brother/sister. Little kids. Babies.) We agree that these three books can be read by people of different ages, but what

about the Bible? (Little kids can't read it, but they could listen while someone older reads. Some older children can read it for themselves. Adults can read it.)

Leader
Message:

The Bible is a very special book. Although it may take us a while to learn to read it, the Bible can never be outgrown. It is a book for all ages. (If this sermon coincides with a service during which Bibles are presented to the children, this might be an appropriate time to do so.)

Closing
Prayer:

We thank you, God, for the Bible and all it means in our lives. As we read from this special book, let the stories through which you speak to all people touch our hearts and minds. Amen.

Materials: Thick, hardbound novel; school reader; child's picture book; Bible; cloth bag or a box.

Scripture
Reference: Psalm 119:105

No. 34

A New Angle   The Bible

Motivation: The leader displays a large triangle.

Activity: The children are asked to count silently the points or corners of this shape.

Guided
Discussion: How many points or corners does this shape have? (Three; the leader counts them to demonstrate.) What is this shape called? (A triangle.) That's correct. "Tri" (spelled *t, r, i*) means three. A tricycle has three wheels. A tripod for a camera or telescope has three legs. And a triangle has three points or corners or sides.

Leader
Message: The Bible tells us that many important ideas in our Christian religion deal with the number three. There were three wise men. Three times Peter denied he knew Jesus. And, of course, there are three parts to the trinity: God the Creator, the Son, and the Holy Spirit. It's interesting that such a simple shape could hold such deep meaning.

Closing
Prayer: God, thank you for all the special meanings you have given us in the Bible. Open our eyes and our hearts, so that we may discover your meanings more perfectly. Amen.

Materials: Large triangle made of some sturdy substance.

***Scripture
Reference:***   1 Corinthians 13:13

Special Delivery The Bible

Motivation: The leader displays a rural mailbox in which a letter has been placed.

Activity: Two or three children are invited to open the mailbox and see if there is any mail. They discover a letter addressed to the leader by name and to "the children."

Guided
Discussion: (None today.)

Leader
Message: We all enjoy getting letters. Sometimes when we are expecting a letter, we check the mail-

box two or three times. We can hardly wait for it to arrive.

Long ago, a man named Paul wrote several letters to the early Christian churches. He offered words of encouragement, he told them the latest news, and he gave them advice about how to follow Jesus. Those who received Paul's letters looked forward to hearing from him. The letters of Paul are included in the Bible.

The letter you found in our mailbox contains some of what Paul wrote to the members of the church in the city of Corinth. Are you curious about what it says? (Leader opens the letter.) These are among his closing words, and I think they will make a good ending: "Try to grow perfect; help one another. Be united; live in peace, and the God of love and peace be with you [JB]."

Closing
Prayer: Dear God, help us to grow more perfect everyday and to live in love and peace with everyone. Amen.

Materials: Rural mailbox, preferably displayed in a freestanding manner (some other container may be substituted if such a mailbox is impractical); envelope addressed to the leader by name and to "the children"; letter containing the scripture citation above or any other appropriate passage from the letters of Paul.

Scripture
Reference: 2 Corinthians 13:11.

On the Outside Looking In

Non-Christians

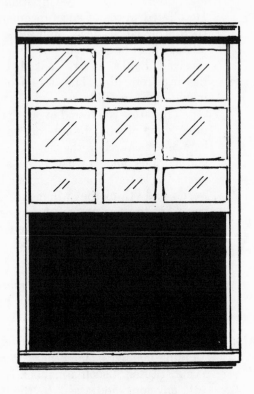

Motivation:	The leader displays a window frame.
Activity:	The frame is held between the children and the congregation, and the children are invited to peek through and tell what they see. (People. My family. Christians. The church.) After two or three children have looked, the frame is put aside.
Guided Discussion:	Have you ever been window shopping? (Yes.) What sorts of things do you see when you are

window shopping? (Toys. Cars. Furniture. Clothing.)

Leader
Message:

Most of us have been window shopping. It is a good way to see what a store has to offer without going inside. Sometimes people who are not Christians go window shopping by looking at churches to see what they have to offer. They look to see what we're doing and what we believe and how we live our lives. Sometimes, they are so impressed by our love that they become Christians too.

But what about those who don't? The Bible says that those who are not against Jesus are for him. It also says that all people are welcome in God's kingdom. In addition, it reminds us not to judge other people, not to decide if they are living a good life or a bad one. It is God's right to judge, not ours.

The important lesson in all this is that we are all—Christians and non-Christians—God's children. As Christians, we have a special duty to see others as they are and, through our love, to invite them to look through the Christian window.

Closing
Prayer:

God, hear our special prayer for those who have not yet found you. We ask in Jesus' name that they be directed to learn of your love. Amen.

Materials:

A small wooden window frame without glass, or a piece of cardboard fashioned to resemble a window frame.

*Scripture
References:*

1 John 4:11
Matthew 7:1

No. 37

A Special Tool — Stewardship

Motivation: The leader displays a small toolbox containing such tools as a hammer, a wrench, pliers, a screwdriver, and a measuring tape.

Activity: With the children seated in a circle, some are asked to choose a tool and tell how it is used. (Screwdriver to repair a bicycle, etc.) After each tool has been discussed, the leader produces a one-dollar bill.

Guided Discussion: How might this dollar be used? (To buy toys. Buy food. Could be saved.)

Leader Message: Money is a tool just like the others we have discussed. If it is used carefully and for the right purposes, money can help people and do good things. If used carelessly, money can destroy things and make people unhappy.

Sometimes in church we hear people talk about *stewardship*. A *steward* is a person who uses money wisely and tries to do good with it. In the church we try to practice good stewardship. Money is a powerful tool, and it is important to use it in ways that will do the most good.

Closing Prayer: Help us, dear God, to serve you in everything we do. Guide us to use money to help others and to promote your kingdom. Amen.

Materials: Toolbox; tools; one-dollar bill.

Scripture Reference: 1 Peter 4:10

No. 38

The Twelve Strokes   The New Year

Motivation: The leader displays a clock that strikes the hour. The leader invites the children to think about the coming (or passing) of the New Year.

Activity: The children are invited to listen carefully and count the number of times the clock strikes. The clock is advanced to strike twelve times.

Guided
Discussion: What does it mean when the clock strikes twelve on December 31, New Year's Eve? (The old year is over. The new year is beginning. It's a new year.) Is there anything special about the number twelve? (It stands for twelve o'clock. It is a dozen. It stands for noon/midnight. Other answers.)

Leader
Message: Twelve is a special number. Do you all remember that Jesus had twelve disciples? Since Jesus' time, we have come to think of all Christians as being disciples, or followers, of Jesus. I am a disciple, so are all of you, and so are the members of this congregation.

When I hear the clock striking twelve on New Year's Eve, I think of the twelve disciples—those special followers of Jesus. As I listen to each stroke of the clock, I think of Peter and John and James and Andrew and Philip and Thomas and Bartholomew and Matthew and James and Thaddaeus and Simon and Judas. (Leader counts the names with his or her fingers.) And just as the last stroke of midnight sounds, I think of myself—that I too am called into a new year and into a new life as a disciple of Jesus.

Closing
Prayer: Dear God, thank you for each new year, for each new day, and for the opportunity to be called into your service. Amen.

Materials: Clock that strikes the hour. Organ or bells may be used if a clock is unavailable or impractical.

Scripture
Reference: Matthew 5:16

Election Day or
The People's Choice Presidents' Birthdays

Motivation: The leader displays large likenesses of George Washington, Abraham Lincoln, and an unknown person.

Activity: The children are invited to pretend that they are voting to decide who will be President of the United States. These three people, they are told, are the ones they may choose from. The children are asked to raise their hands only once to vote. The election is conducted. (Votes may be recorded on a chalkboard or on newsprint.)

Guided Discussion:	Let's talk about the winner, the person who got the most votes. Why was this person chosen? (Already famous. We know him. A great President. I recognized him.) What about this person (indicating the unknown)? Why wasn't this person chosen? (Never saw him before. Not famous. Don't know him.)
Leader Message:	It's interesting that we tend to choose people we know. Sometimes we don't know what to think about a stranger. The better we know people, the more we trust them and depend on them. In church we talk a lot about *knowing* Jesus. When we know Jesus, we find it natural to trust him, and we find ourselves looking to him for help and guidance. I hope you'll all continue to work at knowing Jesus. The best thing about knowing Jesus is, when you know him and vote for him, you're the one who wins.
Closing Prayer:	Jesus, thank you for helping us to know you, and thank you for wanting to know us. Amen.
Materials:	Three large pictures: one of George Washington, one of Abraham Lincoln, and one of a person whom the children will not recognize. (To increase the likelihood that either Washington or Lincoln will be selected, the third person should be a man.) A chalkboard or newsprint to record the votes might be convenient.
Scripture Reference:	Mark 1:16-17

Enough to Go Around Valentine's Day

Motivation:	The leader produces two oversized valentines and announces that the children can help with a problem. The leader explains that the valentines are for friends, but that there are three friends and only two valentines.
Activity:	The children are invited to think about how they might distribute the valentines in a fair way so that no one will have hurt feelings or feel left out.
Guided Discussion:	How can I solve this problem? (Buy another valentine. Give them to your best friends only. Cut one valentine in half. Don't give valentines to anyone.) These are good ideas. If someone is left out, will their feelings be hurt? (Yes.)
Leader Message:	It's no fun to be left out. It's sad to be forgotten when valentines are passed out. It's sad to be left out when teams are chosen in games or sports. It's sad when people forget your birthday.

But I'm happy to announce that when it comes to a very special gift, a very special event, no one gets left out, no one gets left behind. Jesus tells us that, through him, we can enter into the very special gift of God's kingdom. God always has enough valentines to go around.

Closing Prayer:	Thank you, God. You always have enough love to go around. Help us to remember that you'll never forget us or leave us out. Amen.
Materials:	Two oversized valentines (size helps make them visible to the rest of the congregation).
Scripture Reference:	John 3:16a

A Parade

Palm Sunday

Motivation:

Have the children gather at the rear of the sanctuary this time. Explain that they are going to parade to the front of the church. At a signal, recorded march music is played, or the organist may play a processional or a march tune.

Activity:

The children march forward with the leader at the head modeling an enthusiastic step. When they reach the front of the sanctuary, the children should march in a small circle for a time, long enough to get the feel of the experience.

Guided
Discussion:

How did that marching make you feel? (Tired. It was fun. Exciting.) Do you like parades? (Yes.)

Leader
Message:

Let's all sit back now and I'll tell you a story about a parade that started out full of joy but ended on a sad note. After Jesus had been

teaching for a time in small towns, he came to Jerusalem, a fairly large city. When the people saw him coming they were so filled with joy that they spread their coats on the road and covered the road with green palm branches. Suddenly a happy and noisy parade was under way. People were shouting and marching. Everyone was happy.

But as the parade drew near the city, Jesus cried because he knew that sad times were coming. He knew that the city would misunderstand the parade and that his message to the people would not be heeded.

But we have reason to be joyful, because we know Jesus and we understand his message. Let us remember today those who still do not understand.

Closing
Prayer: Dear God, help us to understand the wonderful message of Jesus, that—through him—we are reborn into a new life. We pray for those who are not yet saved. May they hear and understand. Amen.

Materials: Marching music. The children might be supplied with ferns or other foliage representing palm branches. These can be collected at the end of the march.

Scripture
Reference: Luke 19:37-38

Seeing Is Believing Easter

Motivation:	The children are invited to think of a time when they told the truth but were not believed.
Activity:	The children are encouraged to tell about such a time, or the leader may share an experience.
Guided Discussion:	How do we feel when we tell the truth but are not believed? (Unhappy. Like no one believes us. Like no one trusts us. Angry.)
Leader Message:	Sometimes when we experience or see something, we can't wait to tell someone else, especially if it is something really exciting or unusual. And yet, even though we tell the truth, some people don't believe us.

Today we celebrate Jesus' victory over death. People thought Jesus was dead and they placed him in a grave, but he rose and is alive. Those who realized what had happened tried over and over again to convince others that Jesus had risen, but they were not believed. Even the disciples would not believe until Jesus appeared to them.

We need to be patient when we tell others about Jesus. Sometimes the simplest truths are the most difficult to understand.

Closing Prayer:	O God, we believe that Jesus rose from the dead, that he lives today. Thank you for this wonderful truth. Help us to tell others. Amen.
Materials:	None.
Scripture Reference:	1 Corinthians 15:14, 20a, 57

No. 43

Collect on Delivery   May Day

Motivation: The leader displays a May basket and a large freestanding door made of cardboard (or a door may be imagined). The leader invites the children to describe how a May basket would be delivered and what the giver and the receiver are supposed to do. (You sneak up and put it on someone's doorstep; the giver runs away and the receiver tries to catch and kiss the giver.)

Activity: The leader asks for a volunteer to demonstrate the delivery technique. The giver is allowed to go free. The leader acts as the receiver who comes to the door too late to catch the giver.

Guided
Discussion: What happens if you get a surprise May basket and you don't see the person who leaves it? What would you do? (Try and find out

who left it. Look for them. Chase after them. Ask someone.)

Leader Message:

Isn't it wonderful that each year we receive a beautiful May basket from God? Our countryside is one big May basket, filled with beautiful flowers and lovely trees and brightly colored skies and birds and insects and animals, not to mention the sun and the sounds and smells.

And yet when we find this beautiful surprise at our doorsteps we don't even bother to look for the One responsible to express our thanks. We break our necks chasing after one of our fleet-footed friends who leaves us a May basket, but we are seldom so anxious to seek out the Creator of all this Maytime beauty. The next time you see a beautiful garden or tree, think of it as a very special gift from God, and seek God out and give God thanks.

Closing Prayer:

Dear God, forgive us for taking your beautiful world for granted. Help us to realize that you are with us, revealing yourself through your wonderful creation. Amen.

Materials: May basket with flowers, freestanding door made of cardboard.

Scripture References: Psalm 24:1
Psalm 19:1

Glory in the Morning   Pentecost

Motivation: The leader displays some seeds and a small box of blooming morning glories.

Activity: The children are invited to inspect the seeds and the flowers.

Guided
Discussion: How are these seeds and flowers different? (Seeds are small; flowers are larger. Seeds are dark; flowers are colorful. Seeds are hard; flowers are soft.) Do you think it is possible that these flowers came from seeds such as these? (Yes or no, with various reasons.)

Leader
Message: It may be difficult to believe that these beautiful morning glories grew from such tiny, hard, dark seeds. And yet these seeds can change into these flowers.

　　Today we celebrate Pentecost. Pentecost represents a time of change, a time when the disciples of Jesus were greatly changed by an encounter with the Holy Spirit. Just as it is difficult to understand exactly how seeds like these become such beautiful flowers, it is difficult to explain what happened to the disciples at Pentecost. But we know that they did change, and it is important to remember that the seed for change is inside each of us. Each of us can flower into a more perfect Christian.

Closing
Prayer:

Dear God, we thank you for Pentecost and for its mystery. We accept your challenge to change. Just as beautiful morning glories spring from tiny seeds, help us to become more perfect Christians. Amen.

Materials: Morning glory seeds and flowers. Morning glories are recommended because of the small, inert appearance of the seeds and the vigor of the young plants.

Scripture
Reference: Ephesians 4:15-16

No. 45

Stars and Stripes and Fish   Flag Day

Motivation: The leader displays an aquarium or fish bowl with two or three fairly large fish. An easel with a large tablet in place is also available. An American flag can be displayed.

Activity: The children are invited to examine the fish. After a short time, the bowl or aquarium is covered or removed. Two or three children are selected to draw a picture of a fish on the tablet with felt-tip markers.

Guided Discussion: Can someone tell me what a sign is? (A board with writing on it. Like a stop sign. Like a street sign. Like a billboard.) What does a sign tell us? (Various answers. Stop. Go. What town we're in.) Why do we have signs? (To tell people what to do. To identify things. To announce things. So people know where they are.)

Leader Message:	Long ago, Christians were unable to worship without being punished. But their need to worship together was so strong that they continued to meet in secret. So that members of the church would know each other, and so that places of secret worship could be identified, the sign of the fish was used. This sign looked something like this. (Leader draws the traditional fish symbol, or points to one drawn by one of the children, or turns to the next page in the tablet to reveal a pre-drawn sign.) The fish sign was important. It kept early Christians safe.
	It is unfortunate that Christians once had to meet in secrecy and to fear punishment for their beliefs. I am sad to report that in some parts of the world Christians and others are still punished for their beliefs. In America, we live in a free country where another sign, another symbol, guarantees that we have the right to worship openly and without fear. You might say that on Flag Day we American Christians celebrate the stars and stripes and fish all at the same time.
Closing Prayer:	Dear God, thank you for this wonderful country of ours, where we and others can worship openly and freely. Bless our nation and guide us, that we may bring honor to your name. Amen.
Materials:	Aquarium or fish bowl with two or three large fish, easel with large tablet; felt-tipped markers; American flag.
Scripture Reference:	Psalm 33:12

For Every Season   First Day of Summer

Motivation: The leader displays four symbols: a sun face, a rainbow, a snowflake, and an autumn leaf. The children are invited to think about which season of the year—summer, fall, winter, or spring—each symbol might best represent.

Activity: As the leader holds up each symbol, the children are asked to name the season associated with that symbol. (Leading questions might be useful: During what season does it snow? When does it rain a lot to make the flowers grow again? See notes in the materials section below.) After all associations are made, the symbols are put aside.

Guided
Discussion: What season are we in now? (Spring. Summer.) Actually, summer is just beginning. Each of the seasons of the year has special symbols. (Review the symbols and the seasonal associations just completed.) Tell me, which of these seasons is the best? (Various answers.)

Leader Message:	Each of us has a favorite season. Some people like summer. Others prefer winter or fall, and some think spring is best. We may think that some seasons are better than others, but as Christians we know that each season is special in its own way. In fall we celebrate Thanksgiving. In winter we experience the joy of Christmas. In spring we rejoice in the message of Easter, a message so powerful and so wonderful that it stays with us throughout the summer and the rest of the year.
	For Christians, the year is not four separate seasons but a continuous circle, a steady flow of God's love from one month to the next.
Closing Prayer:	Dear God, we thank you for our wonderful world with its flow of seasons—all so different but all part of your wonderful circle of life. Grant that we may experience your love in every season. Amen.
Materials:	Different geographic regions experience different versions of the seasons. Choose symbols that seem most appropriate to your region. If the use of symbols seems too abstract, cut a calendar apart and paste the months associated with each season on four separate sheets of paper, or simply write the names of the months, clustered by season, on four separate sheets.
Scripture *Reference:*	Ecclesiastes 3:1-2

Put It in Writing   Fourth of July

Motivation: The leader displays a framed or otherwise mounted copy of the Declaration of Independence.

Activity: The children are invited to examine this document to decide what it is.

Guided
Discussion: Does anyone recognize this famous piece of paper? (It's the Declaration of Independence.) What's special about it? (It's old. It says our country is free. It started our revolution. Other answers.)

Leader
Message: The Declaration of Independence represents an idea. In the early days of our country, peo-

ple had the idea that everyone ought to have certain freedoms. It wasn't until they put their idea in writing that things began to happen.

I want to show you another important piece of paper that made things happen. (The leader displays a copy of the church charter.) Years ago, the people of this community had an idea. They wanted to establish a church. They put their idea in writing, and now you and I and all the members of this congregation are sitting inside the walls and beneath the roof of that idea.

As we celebrate the idea of our free country this Fourth of July, let's also take a moment to think back and be grateful to the men and women and children who had the idea, put it in writing, and founded our church.

Closing
Prayer:

Thank you, God, for those people who cared enough to found this church. Help us to continue that caring feeling. Amen.

Materials:

Framed or otherwise mounted copy of the Declaration of Independence; framed or otherwise mounted copy of the church charter or other founding document.

Scripture
Reference:

Acts 2:46-47

New Kid on the Block   Back to School

Motivation:	The leader displays a sheet of paper upon which the names of local elementary schools have been written.
Activity:	The children are invited to read this list and think about what all the names have in common. (If there is only one elementary school in your community, put its name on the sheet of paper. In the discussion, ask the children what the name means or other appropriate questions.)
Guided Discussion:	In what way are all these names alike? (They are all names of schools. My school is on the list.) When you go to school this year, you'll probably feel excited and a little nervous. These are natural feelings that we all have

when we begin something new. How do you think people—children and grown-ups—feel when they come to our church for the first time? (Nervous. Excited. Afraid.)

Leader Message: Whenever we begin a new experience, we are naturally a little nervous. We don't know what to expect. Will the people like me? Will I do something wrong? Coming to a new church is much like returning to school. It takes a while to get used to things. When you see a new boy or girl at school, you can help that person feel at home by telling him or her your name and asking theirs, by showing them where things are, and by acting friendly. When you see new people in our church, I hope you—and all of us—will do the same.

Closing Prayer: Dear Jesus, help us to remember that you were once a stranger on this earth. You said that when we welcome someone in your name, it is as if we welcome you. Open our hearts to those who worship with us. Amen.

Materials: Large sheet of paper with the names of local elementary schools printed in large letters. Pictures of the schools might aid the younger children.

Scripture References: Hebrews 13:2a
Matthew 25:35c

A Mask

Halloween

Motivation: The leader invites the children to help solve a mystery. They are told that a mystery person will visit them. They are asked to watch quietly and to try and decide who the person is.

Activity: A person comes forward wearing a neutral (not funny or frightening) mask. The person is dressed in ordinary fashion except for the mask. The person does not speak and remains in view only a few moments. When the person is gone, the children are invited to share their ideas.

Guided
Discussion: Who do you think that was? (Various guesses; the leader should not comment on the rightness or wrongness of guesses.) Why are there so many guesses? Why are we uncertain who the person is? (Person wore a mask. Couldn't see the face.)

Leader
Message: Halloween is coming (has just passed)—a time when many of us dress up in costumes

and wear masks and pretend, for a short time, to be someone or something else. Masks are fun. They can help us imagine and dream and pretend. Masks can also be used to hide from others and from ourselves. Sometimes, even though we don't actually wear a mask, we pretend to be a certain kind of person or to feel a certain way when we don't really want to.

When we hide behind a mask, we may sometimes fool other people, but we can never really fool ourselves and we can never fool God. We all know that we can be better people, better than any mask we might wear. And God knows too. God knows that each of us can be the very best person possible.

Closing
Prayer:

God, help us to be all that you created us to be. Amen.

Materials:

Neutral (not overtly funny and certainly not frightening) mask; person to wear the mask.

Scripture
Reference:

Psalm 139:1-3

Friends in Need Thanksgiving

Motivation:	The leader displays a stalk of corn or a few ears of corn.
Activity:	The children are invited to think about who first had the idea of growing corn for food.
Guided Discussion:	Who do you think first had the idea of growing corn? (People from long ago. Cave people. Farmers. Indians.)
Leader Message:	We may never know who the first corn-grower was, but we do know that when the early settlers of this country were suffering from lack of food, Indians showed them how to plant corn. The settlers thought of Indians who shared the secret of corn as friendly Indians. Later Indians who wanted to keep their lands fought with and killed the settlers. Indians were killed too. The settlers considered the Indians who fought to be unfriendly.

Today we realize that it was not quite that simple. We realize that the Indians and the settlers did both friendly and unfriendly things. Part of the celebration of Thanksgiving is to recall a time of peace and friendship, when people forgot their differences and shared a meal together in love. As we celebrate Thanksgiving with our families and friends, let us hope and pray for a time when everyone in the world can be united in love and in peace.

Closing Prayer:	Dear Jesus, help us to be instruments of your peace. Be with us as we enjoy the plentiful food and family gatherings this holiday season. Help us to give freely to those around us. Amen.
Materials:	Stalk of corn or a few ears of corn.
Scripture Reference:	Psalm 100:1, 4-5

No. 51

A Package Deal   Advent

Motivation: The leader produces a large basket filled with three distinctively shaped and colorfully wrapped Christmas packages.

Activity: As the leader displays each package, the children are invited to speculate about what sort of present might be contained in each.

Guided Discussion: What might be in this package? (Display each. Children offer various answers. At the leader's discretion, the packages may or may not be opened.)

Leader Message: Part of the fun of receiving presents is thinking about what might be inside. We call this exciting feeling *anticipation,* a kind of joyful waiting.

During this season—just before Christmas—we celebrate *Advent,* a time when Christians look forward to the most special gift of all: Jesus. We feel a special kind of anticipation, a joyful waiting. We become excited not only about Christmas, but also about the fact that every day we receive wonderful gifts through Jesus. This year, as you look forward to Christmas and to giving and receiving gifts, think about how wonderful it is to awaken every day knowing that God's gift—Jesus—is always with you.

Closing Prayer: Dear God, thank you for the wonderful gift of Jesus. We look forward to celebrating Jesus' birth, and we pray that our hearts may be filled with the joy of Christmas all year long. Amen.

Materials: Basket with three distinctively shaped and wrapped gifts.

Scripture References: John 1:14-17   Isaiah 40:4-5   Luke 12:37a

No. 52

The Luck of the Draw   Christmas

Motivation: The leader explains that we will have a very special gift exchange. Each child is given a piece of paper and a pencil and invited to write his or her name and place the slip of paper in a paper bag. (The older children can help those who cannot write yet.)

Activity: After all names have been placed in the bag and pencils collected, the leader reaches into the bag to shuffle the names. (Unknown to the children, the bag in which they placed their names has been nested inside a similar bag. As the names are shuffled, the bag containing the names is folded back so that the children will be drawing from the outer bag. The outer bag has been filled with slips of paper with the name "Jesus" written on each.) As the leader shuffles, it is explained that the person whose name we draw and the person who gets our name become part of a

special relationship. Have the children draw and share the name they drew.

Guided Discussion: Whose name did we all draw? (Jesus'.) I must admit that I prepared a special bag ahead of time in order to make a point. Just as we all have Jesus' name, Jesus has our names. That means that we are all part of a very special relationship. The message of Christmas is that the Jesus whose birthday we celebrate is special to us, and that each of us is special to Jesus.

Leader Message: Jesus is actually a gift himself—God's gift to us. When we exchange gifts with one another at Christmas, we share with others the joyful news of Jesus.

Closing Prayer: O God, what a wonderful gift we have received in your Son, Jesus. Help us in turn to give ourselves to others and to celebrate the love of Jesus. Amen.

Materials: Two paper bags; pencils; slips of paper.

Scripture Reference: John 3:16